Lilacs in November

Cover Design by Gingersnap Photography and Laramie Street
Edited by Becky Massey, Garret and Samantha Bonnette

Lilacs In November

Josh, Jenn, Bella, Elijah, Lizzy, Judah-Joy Hope,
Phineas, Arrow

Contents

Preface

Let me introduce myself and my family. I am a mom of 7 beautiful children. Sometimes when I am out and about I get asked if they are all mine or if I am the nanny. They are indeed all mine and I have enjoyed each and every one of them. I feel incredibly blessed to have so many children that I get to raise and invest in.

I am the wife of a gracious and kind man who happens to be my college sweetheart. I have known this man for over half of my life and it just keeps getting sweeter as the years go by. We live in a peaceful home in North Texas with a dog and a lot of fish. At times it feels like our home is cramped and we need more space then I sit back and breathe. Life with all of these lovely people is an adventure and my desire is to embrace each day to the fullest.

Now that you know a little bit about me, I want you to find a comfy chair, your favorite blanket and relax. Pour yourself a cup of your favorite coffee, put on some soft music and let the words from these pages take you on a journey.

This is my story. It is the story of my family and our adventures over the past few years. It is a story of great loss and deep healing. You may find yourself throughout the pages of this journey and feel a tug on your heart. You may feel sadness and grief as well as utter amazement and joy.

My prayer for you is that you will connect with this story somehow. Deep inside, your emotions will be awakened and healing may come to your life. I pray that the words on these pages will be like a sweet hug for you. May you feel a sense of hope and love.

Even though you may be facing great adversity and heartache you are loved and your story is not over. There is a strength within you that is being developed even as you begin to read these words. He knows the journey that you have been on and the tears that you have cried in the secret places. He longs to bring you comfort and peace even in this difficult season. My God has walked with me through the trauma and not left me to fend for myself.

You have been on His mind since the beginning of time. He has thoughts towards you that outnumber the grains of sand on the seashore and the stars in the sky. He is moved by your life and the pain that you have experienced. The Father longs to experience life with you and carry you when you do not have the strength.

There were times over the years where I felt like my heart had become numb. I did not have feeling and did not desire too because the pain was so deep. There were times that I would ask myself if life was really worth living. And somewhere along the way I have found hope. At first it was just a flicker. Eventually that flicker turned into a small flame and then it was a large one that couldn't be contained. Hope has been awakened in my life and my soul. Hope has been the anchor to my journey.

Through this struggle I believe that I have gained the most beautiful strength. I have found hope. Hope has become the anthem for my family and life. I have felt the deepest of emotions that I never knew were possible and connected with God in those moments. I have discovered life is more beautiful when you embrace the pain and face it head on. Beauty can truly rise up from the ashes of death.

This journey has truly been a gift from the Lord. He has been with me every step of the way. He has never left me or kept me stuck in my pain but has given me life. I have seen the human heart bear the burden of loss and the gift of life in the same moment. I have felt heart ache that feels as though someone was ripping my heart out of my chest. And yet in the same moment the spirit of the living God breathed life into my lungs and caused me to live. It is this hope that I have found.

You may be asking yourself how can these emotions be

within the same person? How can you experience life and death in the same moment? Where does this strength and hope come from? And how do I continue to live life when it seems that death is surrounding me?

Death will overwhelm and swallow you if you allow it too. It will be what keeps you up at night and what hangs on when the sun rises. But oh there is a sweet hope that I have found in Jesus.

If you know that there is pain present in your soul you may not know how to work through it. I encourage you embrace that pain. Allow God to walk with you.

Let your heart be stirred and your soul be awakened as your read my story. Open your heart and let the light begin to peak through. It is likened to the rising of the sun on a warm summer morning. When the sun just begins to peak through the window and the light fills the room.

When that light fills the room the darkness begins dissipate and flee. Darkness cannot exist where the presence of light is.

I love what Psalms says about David when he is telling his soul to praise the Lord in the midst of great despair. He tells his soul to look up and trust the Lord. He tells himself to praise the living God. He tells his soul that you will praise the Lord. He commands his soul to reach out and worship the God of Abraham. David was faced with death in his life and when he was desperate for God to move God showed up and moved on his behalf.

When David had no hope he chose to worship His God. He made a choice to worship through his circumstance. Psalm 43:5 says, "Why my soul are you downcast? Why so disturbed within me? Put your hope in God, for I will yet praise, my Savior and my God."

When we begin to worship the Lord in those desperate times we are bringing heaven to earth. We are saying Lord we need your presence to invade our circumstances. Our God is a gentleman and desires that we invite him into our life. He wants to move on our behalf but is awaiting an invitation.

This has been my journey since 2011. Learning to live with

great loss and pain and somehow found hope in the process. Praying that you will see the tapestry of God's goodness in the midst of your journey.

A New Journey
Chapter 1

Let's begin in August of 2010. What a beautiful month of the year. I was in my last year of a rigorous master's program. You see I had decided in my late 20's to return to school to get my master's in counseling. At that time my handsome husband and I had 3 children and were doing well. He was on staff at a church and life was good. We had a rhythm going and we seemed to be moving right along. I was preparing to take on my last semester of classes and then I was doing an internship. I was excited to be on the last part of this journey I could see an end in sight.

One morning I woke up and was not feeling myself. As I began to evaluate my symptoms I quickly realized they were the same symptoms I had 3 other times in my life. I realized that these symptoms were classic pregnancy symptoms. They were the common nausea, fatigue, complete exhaustion, and a gag reflux that acted up when I smelled coffee.

I was a little shocked, elated, scared, fearful, anxious, and mad. I was not ready to be pregnant again. We knew that we would have more children someday but I was on this path to complete school. My dream was to be a counselor and help families. I was at the end of my education and I was not prepared for this pregnancy. I did not have time in my life for another baby this was something I was not prepared to handle.

I realized in those first few moments that life was about to change and I needed to somehow roll with it. I remember the day that I went to visit my husband at work and he was making his lunch. I walked in with our 3 kids and I had the pregnancy test and it was positive. I kind of tossed it in his direction. He had his lunch in one hand and the pregnancy test in the other. I will admit that it was not the most convenient time for me to tell him that we were pregnant again but I was in shock. He was just as surprised as me and he asked the classic question, "How did this happen?"

As time progressed I went to my first doctor's appointment and I remember it like it was yesterday. The memories have been forever etched in my mind. I wore a white linen dress and arrived a bit early. As I got out of the car I remember saying, "I am a little nervous about this whole process." Josh being the supportive guy he is said, "Oh you are just worried it may be twins." We had quite the laugh and then I went to my appointment. I remember just blowing off his comedy because as far as I knew twins had to run in the family line.

My emotions were still all over the place. I was grateful that we were having another child but also upset that it was interrupting my plans. During the appointment I filled out the paper work and stood on the scale to get my weight. Then it was time to do the initial ultrasound. I laid there on the cold table as they put the goop on my belly. The nurse began to show me the images and then she said these words "here is baby A and here is baby B." I was in total shock and amazement. My eyes began to well up with tears that ran down my cold cheeks. I was having twins! I was going to have 5 children. I was going to be overwhelmed. I was going to have twins. I remember telling the Lord how sorry I was that I was not enthused about this pregnancy.

In those first few moments my heart was changed. There was a shift that took place and I no longer wanted my plans for my life. I wanted to surrender to the Lord's plan. I had this desire to be the best mom and to care for these little lives. I felt incredibly special to be given this gift. As the nurse went on she began to tell me how beautiful the babies were and that they were going to be identical twin boys.

It was one of those chance things that happen when the egg splits early on in pregnancy and two babies are developed. I was in complete disbelief as I left the office. I remember walking outside and seeing the bushes and taking a deep breath and thinking that life would be ok. After I composed myself I called my husband and told him the wonderful and surprising news and he thought I was joking. It took him a few moments to realize that I was serious and we were in fact going to be adding two more to our family.

As I am recalling these precious memories I am reminded that I said yes to Jesus and because I said yes to him I can rely on him to walk with me and give me wisdom. Of course, I know how this pregnancy happened but I believe that the Lord had these babies in his plan for my life and for these babies. Proverbs 3:5-6 says, "Trust God with all of your heart, don't try to figure everything out on your own. Listen for God's voice in everything you do, everywhere you go, he's the one who will keep you on track. Don't assume that you know it all. Run to God!" That day in August was one of those days that I said, "Jesus I don't know how I am going to do this but I am relying on you." I felt in those moments that He was so close to me. His heart for me was more than I could comprehend. He tenderly loved me and allowed me to have all of those emotions. He was gracious and kind to me. He was preparing me in those first few days to trust him in deeper ways.

Over the next few months the Lord began speaking things to me about my pregnancy and how I needed to trust him in this process. I had trusted the Lord before but this time seemed to be different. I felt like this pregnancy was not one that I could handle on my own. I had relied on the Lord before with different areas of my life but this time was different. This time I was laying down my desire and asking Jesus to give me his for these little lives. He was so present as I began to trust him. He made himself known and was breathing life into my soul.

During one of my times with the Lord I was talking to Him about Hannah. I was asking the big questions and my heart was broken for her. Hannah was a woman in the Bible who was unable to have children. Her heart was broken and I am pretty sure she felt hopeless and abandoned. She would cry out to the Lord year after year and ask for a son she was specific in her asking. She wanted so much to be a mom and to have a son to give to her husband. And year after year she would not become pregnant. I didn't really understand the gravity of her situation because I felt like every time I looked at my husband I got pregnant.

I knew there was something more that I needed to learn from this story of Hannah. As a mom I wanted to be sensitive to him speaking because His voice is the one that I long to hear. Little did I know that 10 months later the Lord was going to use this story of Hannah to breathe life into my soul.

The Lord had given me a name for one of the twins and it was the name Samuel. As I was reading her story I began to see the faith she had in God. She had this faith that was immoveable. It was not based on her circumstances or even her plans but rather on her God. She knew her God. She was close to Him. I believe that she could feel His presence. She believed in him so much that she made this declaration of faith based in her hope of him. Her character is revealed in her words as she prayed for a son. She prayed for something that she had desired for a long time. She believed that if God would give her a child then he would be faithful to care for heart. She would freely give to the Lord what she had so desperately desired.

I was determined to seek the Lord during this time. I desired to have faith like Hannah, a faith that was willing to ask the Lord for something and then release that very thing back to Him. Hannah believed that God would do what she asked of Him. She also believed that God would care for her heart as she released that dream back to the Lord. This was a new concept for me to embrace but I thought that if God walked with Hannah then He would walk with me.

The months following I would often ask the Lord, "why Samuel" and the Lord would encourage me to try and grasp the heart Hannah had toward Him. I needed to understand that God cares about the desires that we have. I felt as though the Lord was teaching me that I can ask Him for things in life and then I can trust them as I give them back to the Lord. It was during those months that we named them in the womb. We had named them in the womb we had Phineas David on the right of my belly and Zadok Samuel on the left.

The twin's names were ones from the Old Testament and they were ones of power and wisdom. Phineas was a great man who decided to be dedicated to the things of God. In the Old Testament there was a plague that was destroying the Israelites because of their sin. They were bringing the Moabite women into their tents during a time when there was repenting going on in the camp.

Phineas had finally had enough so he went into the tent where two people were having relations and he shish kabobbed them. God told Phineas that because of your righteous act I will stop the plague and bless your lineage. The blessing came years later as Zadok (who was the high priest at the time) was dedicating Solomon's temple. The presence of the Lord fell and brought about a beautiful time of the Lord speaking to His people. The Israelites had not heard the Lord in years so to hear the Lord at this time was a fulfillment of his promise.

Josh and I knew this story and so desired that our boys would be set apart for the Lord. We knew that because they were twins they would have a special bond that none of our other children had. We believed that the Lord had given us their names and were waiting in anticipation for the Lord to use them. This was our heart for our boys. We wanted God's presence to follow them wherever they set their feet.

The pregnancy progressed beautifully. I was gaining lots

of weight and so was my hubby. I think that he had sympathy pounds for me. I mean I was carrying twins and these boys were getting big. Throughout the pregnancy we had numerous ultra-sounds and doctor's appointments so we were able to see the little guys growing. It was a precious time in our family our other children were able to be a part of the process.

There were promises that the Lord spoke to me throughout my pregnancy and I held onto those. They were foundational truths that I would need in the near future.

One of the promises that the Lord had spoken to me was about how he was going to use the boys to bring healing to people's lives. In my mind I had this picture of them heading off to the mission field someday. While there they would pray for people and miraculous healings would occur. I thought how amazing that would be for them to be used in that capacity. I was very excited for my boys and knew that their little lives were going to make an impact. As far as them leaving the home I would not have to worry about that until they were 18 or so.

The days turned into weeks, weeks into months and finally it was time. I had awoken on a Tuesday morning and went about my day. I wore my favorite yoga pants with my black shirt and gray sweater. I had my comfy tennis shoes on and I was ready to conquer this Tuesday. I had a list of things to do. I needed to go grocery shopping, the bank and get my hair cut. A girl has to do what she has to do right? This was my 4th pregnancy so I knew what to expect as it was getting closer. All day long I had contractions but nothing big just steady contractions. I had finally reached 35 weeks so no matter what happened from here on out we were home free.

I managed to make it to 7:30 pm that night when I finally told my husband that I was going to go to the hospital and see what was going on. I told him that if I needed him there, I would call him and he could come. However, he did not do what I asked him instead he wanted to come with me. So we packed our bags and off we went. Once we arrived I realized that this was indeed labor and these babies were coming. I was elated. I had waited for these boys for 8 months. We had prayed over them, named them and had their days planned out even before they were born.

Within just a few short hours I gave birth to two incredibly beautiful boys. They were finally here on March 2, 2011 at 1:07 and 1:08 in the morning. We were so proud of them. I was overwhelmed with joy. I could not wait to see them. As soon as I was able to feel my legs I was down in the NICU to see my boys.

It was early in the morning that they rolled me down the hall in a wheelchair to see my boys. Those were sweet moments that I still remember to this day. It was a beautiful and precious time for me. I remember looking in at their little bodies and thinking how blessed I was to have been given these babies. It was an honor and a joy. They were a wee bit early so they had to stay in the hospital for 8 days.

During those 8 days the Lord would constantly speak love and encouragement to me. He strengthened me to handle the stress of preemie babies, caring for three other children, and recovering from a C-section. His grace was all over us as we tried to figure out this new normal.

We brought our boys home on March 16, 2011. They had matching little outfits with a lion on them. The clothes were too big for them. They looked like baby dolls in their clothes. They were sweet and precious. I just could not stop smiling. There was something birthed in me during my stay at that hospital. There was this gratitude to the Lord for the gift of life. We finally set foot in our home and realized we were complete, We were HOME.........

Home

Chapter 2

I am not sure what your idea of home is but I want to invite you to go down memory lane with me for just a minute. When I was younger much younger than I am now I use to love this Folger's commercial. It would come on around the holidays and everytime I would see it.

I longed for that home and the atmosphere. The quick commercial shows this beautiful white colonial home with a big driveway. The kind of home similar to the home in Father of the Bride. It was peaceful and perfect.

I could imagine the joy that was evident in the family as they sat around the dinner table laughing and enjoying each other's company. The sun begins to peek through the window and you see a parent making coffee early in the morning and then all of a sudden her son comes walking down the stairs. He had surprised her and come home for a visit. The fresh smell of coffee brewing, the warmth of the sun peeking through the windows, and the fresh blanket of snow on the ground outside. It seemed to be absolutely perfect.

This is the kind of home that I had dreamed of my whole life. I wanted to someday have this beautiful home with the kids and my hubby. I always identified with this commercial as silly as it may seem because it represented home. It was a dream I had as a little girl to have a place that was full of peace and hope. I would cry every time the commercial played.

I grew up in a home that was full of contention and eventually my parents divorced when I was in my twenties. That was a journey that has taken me years to work through. So it was of utmost importance for me to have a family that was very much like that perfect home. I wanted that home for my family. I desired to have my children all under one roof with fresh snow on the ground and peace in the air.

In the summer of 2011 we moved into our home. It had a pool in the back yard and enough bedrooms for our big family. We had plenty of space to spread out, but most importantly it was our home. Our family was finally complete and life could settle down for a bit so I thought. At this time our family consisted of our twin boys and 3 other little munchkins, all age 7 and under. Life was good and our home was perfect.

It was a busy August afternoon and I had not showered yet and was in the midst of a huge pile of laundry. It was extremely hot and the temperature was almost 100 degrees. In my house the air was on but it was so humid that you could just feel the air sticking to your skin. In the Midwest this is a typical summer day. This particular day I felt like my life was a whirlwind. I was constantly cleaning, and feeding, and changing diapers. I had to make dinner, do the laundry and nurse my 5 ½ month old twins. Yes, I was exclusively nursing my twins so I felt like I was a cow constantly being milked.

There never seemed to be time for me. I had no time to even process and think about life because I was so overwhelmed with the day to day activities. I was exhausted on all ends and could not see an end in sight. There was little time to shower let alone put on make-up. This was my life from 8am one day to 8 am the next day. It was a life that I had chosen and was fully embracing. I just felt depleted and even a little guilty for being exhausted.

On August 18, 2011 a hot and humid morning as I awoke to the sound of a baby crying I thought wow there is only one crying that means that Zadok slept all night. I left my sleepy husband in our room and walked down the hall half asleep in my summer nightgown I found the most horrific sight. I saw a baby that was black and blue. I felt my babies precious arms and they felt like ice. I picked him up and kissed him thinking that I could somehow revive his body. Those memories are forever engrained in my mind.

Tragedy had struck my home. My son who was once alive was now dead. My home was supposed to be a safe place for sweet memories to be made but it had been invaded by death. Our home had been hit with destruction. Chaos had entered our home and no amount of peace was present. There was only panic and cries for help.

I frantically called 911 and screamed my baby isn't breathing. They said to try CPR. I did. My husband did. Nothing happened. We prayed. Nothing happened. We believed. Nothing happened. We trusted. Nothing happened. We had faith. Nothing happened.

I knew I believed in God and knew that He was a God who healed. Where was my God in those moments? Why didn't He wake me up so I could revive my son? Didn't He love me? How was I going to go on and live when my soul felt like death? These were my thoughts as I was trying to grapple with the events that were taking place around me. I felt like I was in a nightmare and at some point in time I would wake up.

The ambulance arrived within a few minutes. It was early in the morning just before 6 am. I was in my pajamas and my husband was standing in his underwear. Something that you would never see but we were desperate for help. As I walked to the end of the driveway and met the EMT I handed him my precious boy. I pleaded with him to help me. Please help me. Make my son breath again. He was so kind and gracious and said we will do what we can.

As I remember those horrible moments it felt like time was standing still. We couldn't get to the hospital fast enough.

We lived only a few minutes from the hospital and as we were driving I remember passing by one of my favorite homes. I would drive by that house almost daily and at night when their lights were on I would longingly look into their windows. They had this beautiful dining room and it had a huge table and it was always so perfect. This was my idea of what home was. The light was on and everything was so peaceful. I remember as we were on the way to the hospital looking at this beautiful home and wondering if life would ever be peaceful again.

I thought that once we got to the hospital they could administer some sort of lifesaving device and he would live. Maybe it would be like the hospital shows where people are revived and they live. I did not realize that my baby was gone. I was in denial. Reality had not set in and I was at a loss. Death was something for the elderly but not for a baby especially not my baby.

Once we arrived at the hospital we were told to stay in the waiting room. It felt like an eternity and the whole time all I could think was that if they could at least get him to breathe I would be content with that. I just did not want to lose him. He may be a vegetable because of the loss of oxygen but that seemed better than death. Meanwhile I had called a friend who had lost a child a few years prior. She was so amazing. She brought me a sweatshirt and tissues. She was so brave to come and sit with me in the same hospital where she had lost her baby just a few short years prior. Her strength was a gift to me during those first few moments. I never knew the loss that she had endured and the journey that she was on until that day. Her presence was a gift.

Eventually the coroner and nurse came to get us and took us to where they laid our son. He was so tiny in his little onsie laying in that big hospital bed. All alone with no one to comfort him. No one to feed him or change his diaper. I remembered in those moments the day before when I had last changed his diaper and put him in his zoo animal onsie. He was so cute and perfect. During those few seconds the reality began to sink in because he was gone. He was not there. There would be no more cries or diapers. He was simply gone.

They eventually told us we could hold him and say our final goodbyes. My husband did his and then it was my turn. At this point in time I was angry but also knew that my heart was full of gratitude to the Lord. I don't know how those two emotions can exist in the same moment but they did. I was angry at the Lord because my son had died. I did not understand why and how this could happen. However, He is the one who blessed me with identical twin boys. He was the one who gave me this precious gift. This was a great wrestle that I have had to endure. I sat there in that moment and sang a song of thanksgiving. I felt gratitude toward the Lord for giving me twins. I knew that if I turned to the Lord He would give me the faith to trust Him. It was just like Hannah. She asked God for a son and told the Lord that she would give the child back to Him. I knew in those moments that this was my Hannah moment. I felt that if Hannah could trust the Lord with her broken heart then I could trust the Lord with my shattered heart.

The Lord knew that this traumatic event would happen and He had prepared my heart to trust Him months prior. The following is my song to God....

"A place so deep where every breath takes such effort. Waves of emotion are never fading. Jesus bring life and health and hope and peace. Wrap my baby Zadok in your arms so tenderly Thank you for this gift that I got to love."

We left the hospital and went home with only one twin. We had to now figure out this new life. This new pattern that did not make sense. A new pattern that was now different colors and even different kinds of fabrics.

My heart ached for my son that I had to leave at the hospital. I had never left him anywhere unless Josh or myself was with him. Now I had to leave him at the hospital for the coroner to take care of him. I had to figure out how to tell my body that it will only be nursing one baby now. There were diapers that I would not get to change and sleepless nights that I would not experience. When there is only one baby instead of two, I now had to figure out how to fill the time that was empty. I did not know how to take on all of these changes.

I was not prepared for this change. I had never been taught how to grieve the loss of my child. No one teaches you about loss. I had heard of other moms who had lost a child but the closest thing to death for me was losing my grandparents. Although death was difficult when I lost them it seemed right at the time. They were much older and they were ready to go to Heaven. But losing a baby just did not seem right. It did not make sense. It seemed horrific.

I had just gotten into a routine with all five of my children and now life was different. I could not wrap my head around what my next steps were going to be but I did know that my son was with Jesus. I clung onto this hope early on. I remember trying to process my baby in heaven enjoying his new life. My heart was aching for my son but I knew that I needed to trust my Jesus. I felt like the closer I could cling to Jesus the closer I was to my son.

As time went on I had to wrestle with all of the chaos and questions of that morning. I had to come to grips with my new reality. My idea of home had just been obliterated into a million pieces. I was now faced with the why? My desire for Home was still present in my life but I had no idea how to remedy the situation. I was not sure that my life would ever be that picture that I had in my head. Will home ever be a place of peace and hope for me?

First Night as a Family of 6

Chapter 3

As we left the hospital we knew that when we arrived home we would have to tell our other three children. As I walked into our home with one car seat tears were running down my face my heart simply hurt. I felt numb to the world and hopeless inside. I looked like a hot mess with my night-gown on and my hair sticking up. I was wrecked to my core.

We sat the kids down in the living room. They were bright eyed and curious. They did not understand where their brother was. It was in that moment that I saw a side of my husband that was beautiful and courageous. The strength and grace that flowed from his words gave me a glimmer of hope.

He began to tell our kids the story of Elijah and how he went to heaven. Then at the end he told them Zadok had passed away in the night and gone to heaven. The strength that my husband had in that moment for him and for our family was a gift from the Lord. We felt God's grace cover our family.

As I recount those precious hours early that morning I can see that God's hand was on our family. The trauma that took place that early morning is one that would haunt and trigger me for a long time. However, God in his goodness protected my children from experiencing any of the trauma. His grace walked with us. His covering was on our family in a way that is unexplainable.

He protected my children from the horror of the ambulance

and the loud screaming. They have no recollection of those moments before the sun came up. They were fast asleep. How good is our God that He would cover and protect our family.

I believe that early that morning the Lord covered my children's ears and kept them sleeping peacefully until the sun had come up. I believe that this is what the Lord did for our family in the brokenness that we walked through "He who dwells in the shelter of the Most High, Will remain secure and rest in the shadow of the Almighty." We did not know how to rest and find security but our God was so good. He met us from the moment tragedy hit and continues to meet us to this very day.

Over the course of the day we had many people in and out and did not have much time to process the tragic events of that morning. It all happened so fast. We had family and friends come and visit and bring food. We had so much food that Josh and I went out and bought a freezer the day after our son passed away.

It was so strange how food brought comfort in that time. I am not sure how food can bring comfort when you have lost so much but it did. We had food for all of our visitors and our family. The food that was brought was a way for people to meet our tangible needs.

Our home was filled with the voices of those who loved our family. We were able to feel the tangible hands of Jesus. We were surrounded by such a heavenly presence even in the midst of our loss.

Then everyone cleared out for the evening and we were alone. Our kids were asleep and we were alone. We now had to deal with the sadness that was in our souls.

It was in that moment that my strong husband got his guitar out and invited me to worship our Jesus. Josh had an inner strength that was so evident that night. He knew that he could not carry his family but he trusted in a God who was capable to carry us.

Hannah had trusted God to care for her and because she trusted Him I believe that He met her in her vulnerable moments. She knew that she could not make it happen on her own so she trusted in God and knew that he would care for her heart along the way.

We sat there on the living room floor with an empty house all around us pouring out our heart to Jesus. It was on this same floor 12 hours before that I was on my knees crying out to Jesus to breathe life into my lifeless son. Now I was on my knees crying out to Jesus to comfort my broken heart. I believe that it is in the places where we are most vulnerable that Jesus is able to do the most intimate work.

My heart was broken. My life felt hopeless. My dreams were shattered. My life was His. I had given my life to Jesus. I had seen him do some amazing things over my life. He had given me an amazing marriage. He had given me children and an incredible husband. He had provided abundantly for our lives. If He had done all of these precious things for me why wouldn't He meet me in these moments as I worshipped and heal my heart?

As we were worshipping I remember the Lord asking me this question. "Will you trust me in this process of healing or will you turn to the world?" I knew in my soul that I had to choose the Lord. There was an urgency that arose in me as I began to answer him. A determination that I was going to choose Jesus. Not only was I going to choose Him I was going to trust Him for every aspect of my healing process. I was going to have to choose him over and over. I was going to cling to him for life and breath. There was no other place for me to turn but to him. He had sustained me and He was the only true hope that I had.

During our time of worship there were songs that Josh had written 10 years before that evening. These songs were specifically written for that night. They were the words that my husband had penned years prior. Those words were for this night as we sit in our living room crying out to the Lord. Of course, we had sung them over the years but they had never felt so real then they did that night. That night they came to life and were healing to our souls. Those words were God breathed for our souls on the evening of August 18th.

God showed up even before the day my son passed. A few weeks prior my husband had ordered a guitar and it was on back order for 6-8 weeks. However, the Lord knew that my son was going to pass away and He also knew that my husband needed his instrument. My husband is a worshipper and his guitar is one of the ways that he leads in worship. My husband has an amazing voice but there is something that changes in the atmosphere when he plays his guitar. It is as though he is joining heaven's angels and bringing others with him. A few days prior to that horrible day my husband received his guitar in the mail. It had come early. We may make plans for our life but it is the Lord who truly directs our steps. The Lord had directed our steps and provided for us that evening. My husband was able to get his guitar out and worship our God.

Our first night as a family of 6 was difficult and extremely sad. We went to bed late that night and honestly I don't remember getting much sleep. I could not get sleep because I was worrying about my son breathing. I was so afraid that he would stop breathing in the night and I would not be able to catch it. I had put a monitor under his new bed and had moved his crib into our master bedroom. I thought that if I could stay awake then I could prevent any further trauma. I eventually fell asleep but I woke up the next morning at the same time my son was pronounced dead the day before.

This night is one that I will never forget. I believe that Josh and I were able to face some things in the first 24 hours of our loss. We chose to trust Jesus in the midst of our pain. We believed that He would do what He had promised in our lives. We chose to trust Him with all of our unanswered questions. I did not quite understand how to walk out this process of healing. There were moments when I had difficulty processing all of my feelings. I had to trust that God would be what I needed as the journey went on.

The next morning I had awakened at 5:48 am a friend had texted me. She did not know that it was the exact time my son had passed away the day before. She just told me that she was thinking about me and felt like she needed to send me a verse of encouragement. It was one of the most beautiful experiences even in the midst of my pain. I had thoughts that morning of extreme anxiety and her Scripture was very specific to my thoughts that I had been thinking. I felt like my pain had been seen and the Lord was telling me that he was with me through that process.

How good is our God that He would prepare a way for us to begin the grieving process and to sustain us when it got too difficult. God was with us when we lost our son. He was so present during that time and continues to be present in our lives. He has never promised a life free of pain and sorrow just that He would be present in the process. He has made a way and sustained us. He has given us a hope for the future. He has made himself so present that people recognize that God is doing a miraculous work.

I remember the sweet presence that entered our living room on that evening. It was sweet and peaceful. It felt like home. There was a heaviness that lifted and a peace that rested over our house. We sat on the living room floor with our living twin sleeping and worshipped. I felt like my husband was playing with all of his broken pieces. This worship was a beautiful thing to be a part of. There is beauty in the broken pieces.

"In the Palm of Your Hand," is a song that
my husband had written years before this tragedy.

In the palm of your hand, that's where I will be, because that's where your holding me. Safe and secure I will endure through life's uncertainty. Though I walk through the fire I am surrounded by flames. I know I am in the center of your gaze. Where can I go that you are no there, where can I run that you won't find me. Wave after waves crashes over me I know they won't over take me. Cause in the palm of your hand that's where I will be. . . that's where your holding me."

It is Well

Chapter 4

It is well with my soul.. . . .When I hear these words it makes my heart ache and stomach tighten. I feel that when I hear this song I ask myself this question, "Will it be well with my soul?" This is a difficult question to answer because it always makes my heart ache. I have to dig deep in my soul and commit to trusting Jesus with this heart ache.

We chose to play this song "It is Well," at our sons viewing at the funeral home. These words were never so true then when we decided to use them as our anthem. There was great grief in the depth of my soul, that can only be filled by the presence and healing power of the Lord. I had never known heartache like this before. I never understood what it was like to lose someone so close, someone who just days ago was nursing at my breast. The ache in my heart was like a stabbing pain in my chest.

The child that I had carried for nine months and given birth too. The child that I had dreamed about their future and how the Lord would use them to bring Him glory. The depth of my heartache was great and felt overpowering at times, but there was also a deep work that the Holy Spirit was about to do in my life.

The next few days were a blur as my husband and I made preparations to burry our son. We had so many decisions to make for the arrangements. On August 19th we had to meet the funeral home and begin making final decisions for our son. The funeral home was amazing and so gracious. I had all of these emotions running through my mind. I did not even want to have a funeral. I just wanted to take my living children and my husband and run away. However, that was not an option. I had to face this pain head on and begin the process of walking it out.

How do you go from the daily grind of raising a family to preparing a funeral for your child? This was the most excruciating event that Josh and I had ever planned.

I felt like we had been thrown into the middle of the ocean and told to swim to shore. We had no idea where our location was or how far it was from the shore, but the only way to get to the shore was to swim. There were times when swimming wasn't enough though because we were now drowning.

A good friend had told us that grief is like a storm. In the beginning it is very intense and the storms come often and then as time goes on the storms become less intense and less often. The next morning as I was taking a shower I had my first of many storms. The pain was as though some one was suffocating me.

It was intense and overwhelming. I remember dropping to my knees in the shower and telling the Lord that I cannot breathe. I can't do this. I don't want to do this. I felt like I wanted my life to end because the pain was so intense. There was a razor in the shower and I thought if I cut myself maybe I will just bleed out and die. It was in that moment that I felt the Lord breathe life into my soul. I felt my lungs begin to breathe and I stood up. I felt this heaviness in my soul get a little lighter. I knew that Jesus had thrown me a rope. This rope was connected to Him. He was the anchor to my soul. He wasn't going to let me die. He was going to walk with me and as soon as I cried out to him He would show up. He was bringing me back to shore.

The day finally came when we had to begin the viewing and funeral events. The preparation was very difficult to say the least.

We were not prepared for this event in our lives. When we

got married we were so naïve. We had never faced anything like death. My husband and I both had grandparents pass away but it was not the same. We had prepared for the funeral but the emotional aspect of this event was incredibly difficult.

This was by far the most excruciating of all of the processes. I did not want to have a funeral. I did not want to live or even breath in that moment. All I wanted to do was die. I felt like everyone else was going on about their life and no one knew my pain.

It sounds really crazy but when we were finally able to see our son at the viewing Josh and I just laughed. People probably thought we had lost our minds. I remember looking at him and thinking he looks like a clown with all of that makeup on him.

We had not lost our minds we just knew that our son was no longer here. His body was present but his spirit was with Jesus. He was never going to know pain or heart ache. He was now living with the Lord and experiencing heaven. This brought peace to my momma's heart. In those moments the sweet presence of the Lord entered into our lives like never before. We could tangibly feel him. He was giving us the strength to carry on and laughter was just the beginning. It truly was well with my soul because I knew Jesus was holding my soul together.

November Blossoms

Chapter 5

Lilacs are one of the most beautiful flowers that I have ever smelled. They have an incredible sweet smell and some would liken it to the smell of heaven. As a child I had a lilac tree growing my backyard. I would often cut the branches off and put them in water so I could enjoy the smell in my bedroom. I think I cut so many flowers that I may have destroyed that beautiful tree. They were so perfectly created. I absolutely love them.

Flowers were a happy place for me when I was a child they would bring a smile to my face. When I was young I took piano lessons from a teacher who lived down the street. My piano teacher lived in a house that had an English garden in the back. It was gorgeous. Her family would spend hours tending to this beautiful garden.

I would often walk through her garden and smell the flowers. It brought this intense joy to my life. The smells would bring peace to my soul and I always imagined myself getting married in a garden like this beautiful one.

Flowers are what the Lord used to show me He loved me when I was young and they are what He used as I was grieving the loss of my son.

It was a fine November day in 2011 that something extraordinary happened. I went along with my usual schedule. I had a play group, a lunch date and then a few meetings. I ended the evening with our house full of the aroma of coffee and the sound of sweet conversation from a group of young adults.

As I reflected on my day with all of its familiarity there was one significant event that occurred. This event may have gone unnoticed had it not been for the impact that it made on my life. You see earlier that evening I was outside playing with the kids. I was enjoying their laughter and the sweet smell of fall. I decided that since I was in such good spirits I would attempt to walk the same path I took the morning that my sweet Zadok passed away.

This path is one that my husband and I travelled every week when we take the trash to the curb. I would often take this path and try not to remember the dreadful morning of his passing. This path was very difficult and rather unbearable.

As I began to take those first few steps I started asking the Lord to begin a newness in me. I needed him to help me take these steps and carry this heavy burden. I started to ask the Lord to heal my heart and give me some new memories.

In those moments He did give me some new memories. He not only gave me some wonderful moments with my son He showed me something beautiful.

You see I love lilacs, the smell of them is breathtaking. While walking I saw an ordinary bush to my right side. This bush had been in our yard since we moved into the house the previous summer. We never noticed any life in the bush but were too busy to remove it over the summer. My hubby decided to let it be until the next spring he wanted to see if there was any life left.

As I looked at the bush that fall day I realized that it had flowers on it and they were blooming. This bush had bloomed just for me, there was life in it afterall.

So I decided that I would pick the two blooms that it had and place them in my kitchen so I could enjoy the sweet aroma. I was amazed that the bush that looked dead was actually alive. It was simply waiting for the right time to bloom.

As I was doing some research on lilacs I came across a lady who said that lilacs will sometimes bloom in November if they have gone through a stressful summer. Our family had certainly endured a stressful summer after the loss of our son. I believe that the Lord was showing me that there is beauty and life even when things look dead.

When I think about the significance of those beautiful flowers I think of how amazing and big our God is. No one else knew that I loved lilacs or that they brought me peace. No one knew that those flowers brought me joy in my soul.

On that chilly day when I asked the Lord for new memories He gave me such a sweet gift. He knew my thoughts that day and answered my cry for help. This was such a beautiful treasure for me to be known by my God. He told me He loved me and that where there was once death He was bringing life.

In the Old testament there is story where Sarai and Abram were desiring a child and they were not able to conceive. Sarai decided to take matters into her own hand and had her handmaid, Hagar, marry her husband. She eventually conceived and gave birth to a boy named Ishmael. During Hagar's pregnancy she began to resent Sarai. As a result she was unfairly treated. Hagar ran away and was found by an angel in the desert. It was there that she knew that God had seen her. He had seen her pain and was present with her in those moments.

"El Roi" is the God who sees me. This was important for Hagar because it was specific to her situation. She was seen by the God of the universe. Our God is a God who sees. Genesis 16:13 "Hagar named the Lord who spoke to her, You are the God who sees me, O Lord you have searched me and known me." (NIV) How good is our God that He would see Hagar in her desperation and bring an answer to her question.

There are times in my journey where I have felt as though the Lord showed me that I was seen. Those lilacs were a reminder for me that Jesus sees my pain and is walking with me and giving me strength. Lilacs in November bloomed just for me!

Life Moves On

Chapter 6

It was the end of November 2011 and we were still struggling with grief and trying to find a new normal. It was a daily struggle to sort out our emotions individually and as a couple and then try to parent our kids. This was a challenging season for us because there were stressors on every side. What we did not know was that our world was going to drastically change yet once again.

My husband had been employed as a pastor for over a year and a half and at Thanksgiving of 2011 he was told they were going to do away with his position. We were told he would have until the end of December, which was a month away to find another job.

This felt like another death to our family. We were still trying to manage our grief and be somewhat coherent for our children and now we had to process finding employment and possibly moving from our home.

We had lived in Illinois for almost 5 years at the time. We had bought a house in the summer of 2011just before Zadok had passed away and we were putting down roots. So, when Josh lost his job it felt like there were sharp pieces of glass that shattered all over our floor. I was not sure what to do in those moments. It was a very dark time for our family.

The grief of losing our son was excruciating and unbearable at times. Here we were just trying to figure out our new life with our family of 6 and now the rug was pulled out from us.

As dark as those days were for our family and the new challenges that we now had to face I cannot help but remember the sweet times I had with the Lord. I felt His presence as we faced all of those challenges.

During the evenings I would sit and watch the sunset from our living room floor each night. I would watch Phineas sit with his blocks and books and play. He would smile and laugh. He brought so much joy to my broken heart.

The sunsets during this time were incredibly beautiful and were absolutely breath taking. I would imagine that the sunset was heaven. I would think of Zadok and how much fun he must be having in heaven. Thinking of the joy and freedom on his face brought a smile to mine. It seemed to ease the pain just a bit. I found so much comfort during those difficult first months as I sat by my window

I spent a lot of time with my children in those months following his death. Sometimes it was out of fear of losing one of them as well as wanting to invest myself into something that matters. I felt like my kids, my husband and loving Jesus is all that mattered to me during that time in my life. I was a mother hen as I gathered my family together.

Most evenings were spent with each other and simply taking in the precious time that we had together. I learned that time was a precious gift and I wanted to make the best use of the time I was given. Time is a precious gift and I simply wanted to keep my family together.

During those late months of November and December of 2011 we began to look for ministry jobs. We knew that as of January we would be out of work and need to find new employment. If I can be honest I was angry and upset. I did not want to move I had a support group and could not imagine leaving. I did not know how I was going to cope.

One day as my husband and I were talking I began to hear his heart and the ache that was within him. I heard him say, "I can't live here because all around me resembles death." As he was speaking I remember being filled with compassion for him in those moments.

That day when he told me that he could not stay in Decatur my pain didn't seem to be as important as my husbands in those moments. So we began the difficult process of finding employment outside of our home.

My sweet husband and I had a healing journey that was very unique. I would liken it to a beautiful ballroom dance. I call it beautiful because this journey was led by the Lord. There were times in our grief journey when I would take the lead and invite the Lord into our process. Then the tables would turn and my husband would be the one leading and I would follow. On a daily basis we would ask each other how we were doing with grief. We had to be open and transparent about our process. I believe that because we faced the pain with transparency we were able to work through the process.

As I look back on that transition I have a big smile now because I know that God was guiding our steps and leading my husband. I could not see the process as I was walking in it but now I see. There was a freedom that was released in our marriage as I trusted my husband with our family. I saw him care for our family with such gentleness and wisdom. Even when he did not have the answers he still guided with such grace.

I like to control everything around me so relinquishing control of our family to my husband was a big decision, but it was the only decision. I knew that my husband wanted so much for our family and I fully trusted his ability to hear the Lord directing us.

It was in March of 2012 that we decided to move from

Illinois to Marshfield, Massachusetts to pastor a small church. We had decided that our move day would be in April which gave us very little time to pack up our home and sell it, but we knew that it was the right timing. As soon as we put our home on the market we got an offer and we accepted it the day before we moved across the country. The guidance of the Lord was extraordinary.

Life is a process and no matter where you are in the process it takes time and patience. This process of moving across the country was going to take great strength and vision. What we did not know as we pulled out of our driveway was the adventure that was awaiting us on the East Coast. We did not know the great healing and the beautiful memories that awaited us as we stepped out. There was a beautiful journey that awaited our family as we ventured into unknown territory.

Once we arrived in Massachusetts we quickly found a new routine. That routine included going to the beach as much as we possibly could. I love the beach it is my safe haven. The beach became the place where I found God and He was my counselor. Every trip to that precious ocean was food for my soul.

Growing up in Maryland I would go to the beach every opportunity I could. I love to sit on the shore and hear the waves crashing on the shore. Then there is the smell that simply takes my breath away. As I breathe in the salty air I am instantly relaxed and all I smell is heaven. I feel at home when I am at the beach. It was my happy place when I was a kid and now it was my happy place as an adult. I believe that the Lord knew that I needed this time in Massachusetts more than I did.

I tried to go to the beach a few times a week. I would pack up my van with our little red wagon, the umbrella, the cooler with all kinds of food, water bottles, a bag of beach toys and 3 beach chairs. It was quite a sight when my kids and I would roll up with all of our stuff. There were times when I had so much stuff that people would come and help me through the sand to get to the water's edge.

Once we arrived at the beach we would set up and the kids would play. We would find clams and snails and crabs. There were so many adventures that my kids had on the beach. Sometimes I would sit on shore and just watch the waves roll in. The sweet smell of the sea was life to my tired body. It rejuvenated every part of my being and allowed me for a minute to connect with something bigger than my sadness. The crash of the waves as they hit the shore were like a lullaby. It soothed even the deepest parts of my soul. It was in those few short months that healing happened because I sat on the shore. I sat on the shore and breathed in the sea.

In this journey I have found that sitting on the shore and taking in the sites sooths the ache of my heart and brings peace. I found peace on those beaches in Massachusetts. I found a renewed hope for life. I found my smile as I watched my children explore the coast. There was a joy that began to reside in my soul as I saw my kids build sand castles and find crabs. The beach was my healing.

People often say that they find themselves at the beach and I would have to agree. I found myself on the shores of the ocean as I trusted Jesus with my heart and soul. Our season was a beautiful one because it was directed by the Lord. There were many tears shed on the shore of the ocean. Eventually though the waves and storms became less intense and less often. Instead of king fearful of what was to come I could embrace the storms and allow the Lord to heal me.

Grief

Chapter 7

After I lost my son I realized that grief was something that I needed to familiarize myself with. It was going to be a new way of life as I navigated through my loss. I felt like life had changed in an instant and I was facing a new reality. This is a reality that I was unfamiliar with, I had only read about people who had faced great grief but never experienced it myself.

I remember reading stories about people who had lost a child or a spouse and it always seemed to strike a chord in my heart. I felt deeply for them and did not understand how they could have hope in the process. There was always something intriguing as I watched people grieve. That something was the hope that they had and the beautiful resolve for life.

There have been times throughout my journey when grief was so great that death seemed as though it would bring some relief. Grief has a way of tricking you to believe that death may be your only hope. At best grief was just a tool to get me through the most difficult time in my life.

I never thought that my life would be interrupted by grief. We had healthy kids and the thought of SIDS never crossed my mind. When I was in the hospital with my twins I had received a pamphlet from the hospital when we were discharged. To my knowledge we were out of the danger zone with our twins. I did not think that death was something that would interrupt our family.

There is a saying that Forest Gump says, “life is like a box of chocolates you never know what you are going to get.” I feel like grief and death are like this. You never know what or how grief is going to affect you. Over the years there have been times when I was overwhelmed with loss. My heart would ache in an incredible way that made my whole body hurt. As I was going through those difficult times I realized that I would need to embrace the pain if I was going heal.

I had to acknowledge the grief and let it work its way out in my life no matter how painful it was. I remember there were times I would be shopping in a store and I would see something that caused me to remember my son. It was always the little things that would bring me to tears.

No one knew what I was going through or why I was crying. It was in those moments that I asked the Lord to be with me and bring me peace. I did not know the proper way to grieve I just knew that in my grief Jesus would make a way for me. He would give me strength to take the next step in my journey. He would give me hope in my soul that life would go on after death.

A wise man shared this with me when my son passed away. “Grief is like waves that are very intense and come often in the beginning and then as time goes by the waves become less intense and less often.” Sometimes those words were all I heard as I clung on to HOPE.

As I was going through this process I wish there was a book that I could have read that would have given me the exact steps to take to feel better or rather to skip the whole process. However, there is no cookie cutter plan to work through grief. Grief comes and Then once you follow these steps the process is over and life is back to the way it was before the loss. However, grieving does not work like that.

It affects everyone in different ways and at different times. Someone losing a parent in their 80’s is different than me losing my son at 5 ½ months old. I was on my own journey of grief and I had to walk through every heart ache, every tear and pain. I had to figure out a way to work through the pain and not avoid it.

As I was going through this process I wished there was a book that I could have read that would have given me the exact steps to take to feel better or rather to skip the whole process. However, there is no cookie cutter plan to work through grief.

However, grieving does not work like that. It affects everyone in different ways and at different times. Someone losing a parent in their 80's is different than me losing my son at 5 ½ months old. I was on my own journey of grief and I had to walk through every heart ache. I had to figure out a way to work through the pain and not avoid it, because if I avoided this pain it would eventually consume me.

We were not created to deal with grief but because of this world we are faced with it on a daily basis. Our creator crafted us to walk in close relationship with Him so that we could hear his sweet voice. In the Garden of Eden when Adam and Eve walked with God. His ears were turned toward them. He longed to hear them speak and spend time with them. He had created this beautiful world just for them to enjoy. Once sin entered the world they were disconnected from their Creator. The very one who breathed life into their bodies was no longer close with them. As I think of the longing that God must have had for his Creation to be connected with him. This is where grief entered and man was separated from the Lord. God's heart was broken for His creation.

He desires that we become so closely connected with Him that we can hear his very whispers. I have experienced the very whispers of my God through my journey of grief. His sweet voice has been a lullaby to my ears. The songs that He has sang to me have given me the very breath that I need to continue on this journey.

Psalm 42:1 "As the deer pants for streams of water, so my soul pants for you, O God. My soul thirsts for God, for the living God." This was the cry of my heart day and night. A deer will stop and drink when it feels safe, this was where I found my safety. My safety and security was found in my Creator, I longed for the Lord. I needed God to show up in my life and walk me through this grief. I longed for God to provide a way for me through this process because without Him I would surely die.

The grief that my husband and I have had to endure and work through has been excruciating. Our family has learned that as we embrace the pain we find healing and peace in our God. He never ceases to meet us and show us more of his character and goodness. Our son's death was not caused by God but He will use this horrible tragedy to heal our hearts and bring people to Himself. We chose early on to set our hearts on the Lord and to trust Him with our healing. He has met us at every point of desperation and sadness and brought us hope.

I may have some scars all over my heart but I have a closeness to the father that I would not trade for anything. I know that I hear the Lord speaking to me and I know He hears my cries for help. I will leave you with this picture… Imagine a sweet little girl with blue eyes and curly hair she has just scraped her knee. Off in the distance you see her dad scoop her up and place her on his knee and he begins to wash her face and hands. He then looks at her little scrape and carefully cleans it out and places her favorite bandaid on it. He gives her a super big bear hug and you see her nestle into his arms. She stops crying because the pain is no longer present and she begins to smile.

This is a picture of what the Lord would do for me every time I cried to him for help. He would pick me up and clean me off then hold me until the pain subsided.

Held Psalm 91

Chapter 8

There are specific events that happen in my life that are so engrained in my brain. One of those being the day that I was holding my boys in my arms as I was sitting in my rocking chair.

I had this cream colored fabric rocking chair that was a little old and tattered. It had stains from all of my children and nice permanent black marker stripe on the back of it that one of my kids thought was a good idea. It did not look the best but it got the job done and it was so comfortable. There was even a stool for my tired feet.

This rocking chair was my favorite piece of furniture that we had in our home. I had received it one year for Mother's Day. I absolutely loved it. Every time that I sat in it I felt like time stood still. It reminds me of people who live in the south. They sit on their front porch and drink their sweet tea while rocking in their chairs. Time seems to stand still and they take in the beauty that is around them. Conversations happen in rocking chairs. Children sit on their mammas laps and have stories read to them in rocking chairs. Babies are nursed and given sustenance for life in rocking chairs.

As I would sit in my rocking chair, all of the stress and anxiety, fear and worries of my world seemed to slip away with each rock. It was my sacred space. It is where I went to hold the most beautiful gifts in the world, my children. I loved my rocking chair.

It was midmorning and I had just finished feeding my boys so they were happy. I sat in my stained and torn rocking chair and was just breathing in these sweet moments. I was holding my precious babies. And I began to feel so overwhelmed with gratitude for their little lives. I felt honored to have been given twins. I truly felt like they were a gift from the Lord to me.

This was such a special time for me as I sat in my chair. Over the years I have realized that my chair had become a sweet and sacred place. This is where I have heard some of the most beautiful words that have given me life.

One day I was thinking about the words that the Lord had spoken to me about my boys and I began to tear up. Excited about the adventures that they would go on and how they were going to be close as they grew up. I couldn't wait for the day when they would be running around the house getting into trouble because let's face it they were twin boys. I could imagine them climbing trees together and playing cops and robbers. This was my dream for them to be close. This was going to be a special season for my family as we embraced all of the new things these boys were going to do.

As I sat there in awe of my boys I remember that the Lord had said that these boys would be used for healing. He was going to use them to bring healing in people's lives. I thought for sure they would grow up to be missionaries and go overseas somewhere sharing the Gospel. I couldn't help but have a little ache in my heart because I knew someday they would be off on their own adventures. But for the time being I was thankful for the time I had to nurse and rock them in my precious rocking chair. I was embracing these moments because I knew that it would not last forever.

I thanked the Lord for letting me be their mama and was overwhelmed gratitude that I would get to raise twins. I told the Lord that He could use these boys in whatever capacity He chose to use them in. I fully trusted Him and His plan and purpose for their lives. This was on a hot Tuesday morning on August 16th, little did I know the events that would take place just a few days later.

I kept thinking this was a dream and that life was not playing out like this. Only to find that this was reality for me. I was sitting in a hospital room with a nurse, a coroner, and two cops. My husband and I were told that this was our opportunity to say our final good bye. The walls were white and cold. The only color in the room was the little animal onsie that I had put on my son the night before. I remember it so perfectly. I loved that little onsie. I loved my son.

The nurse handed me my son and I sat on the edge of the rocking chair. I could not bring myself to rock my dead child. I thought my son is not here, he is with Jesus. This is just his cold hard body. I had to grapple with the emotions and the shock of these events. Just 12 hours before I was nursing him because he was fussy. I was changing his diaper and dressing him in his onsie.

This was the most difficult time in my life. I felt the pain wanting to creep into my life and I knew that I did not want to feel anything in these moments. I knew that I had to walk through this process but it was so uncomfortable. I felt my heart sank and I wanted to puke all at the same time. This was not easy for me to accept and I had no idea how to deal with all of this change.

Even as I write these words the emotions are so raw. It is one thing to have walked through them and it is another to revisit and remember. To stay in the moment and allow myself to feel such raw emotion is painful, but it can be so healing as to embrace the pain. Pain does have a purpose at times in our life. With all of the children that I have given birth too each one came into this world with some sort of pain.

I so value those precious memories in my old rocking chair because those were a gift from the Lord. I found myself wanting those days with my boys to return, but they could not. I had a new reality and that was one of complete loss and utter brokenness.

Looking back on that day in the hospital in my rocking chair the Lord was the one doing the holding. He was holding me as I was holding my son. I may have not been able to rock with peace and joy but I could embrace the pain and invite Jesus into those moments. I love that Jesus allowed me to hold my babies all while He was holding me.

The day after we lost our son I woke up singing a song called, "Held." It is a song by Natalie Grant. I was just beginning to learn what it meant to be held. I think for so long I had held everyone else but it was now my turn to be held. We chose this song to play at our son's funeral. I had heard it before but it wasn't until that moment that it clicked. The song was written for a lady who had lost a child at two months. A lady who probably knew the Lord. She could not understand how her son could die at such a young age. This song spoke to my heart then and continues to speak to me now.

Jesus held me in my pain and continues to hold me now. He keeps me. He surrounds me. He comforts me. He sustains me. He leads me. Pain does not control my circumstances or my life. Instead it has challenged me to dig deep and trust God more. Pain can drive you away from the very presence of a God who loves you but if you will choose to trust Him in the process He will draw you so close. There is an intimacy that I have with Jesus because of my pain. I trust Him with my family and my life. He knows me and sees me and loves me in tangible ways.

I continue to cling to him for strength and allow him to hold me and my family in the palm of his hand. He is a good God.

Psalm 91

1 Whoever dwells in the shelter of the Most High
will rest in the shadow of the Almighty.
2 I will say of the Lord, "He is my refuge and my fortress,
my God, in whom I trust."

3 Surely he will save you
from the fowler's snare
and from the deadly pestilence.
4 He will cover you with his feathers,
and under his wings you will find refuge;
his faithfulness will be your shield and rampart.
5 You will not fear the terror of night,
nor the arrow that flies by day,
6 nor the pestilence that stalks in the darkness,
nor the plague that destroys at midday.
7 A thousand may fall at your side,
ten thousand at your right hand
but it will not come near you.
8 You will only observe with your eyes
and see the punishment of the wicked.
9 If you say, "The Lord is my refuge,"
and you make the Most High your dwelling,
10 no harm will overtake you,
no disaster will come near your tent.
11 For he will command his angels concerning you
to guard you in all your ways;
12 they will lift you up in their hands,
so that you will not strike your foot against a stone.
13 You will tread on the lion and the cobra;
you will trample the great lion and the serpent.
14 "Because he loves me," says the Lord, "I will rescue him;
I will protect him, for he acknowledges my name.
15 He will call on me, and I will answer him;
I will be with him in trouble,
I will deliver him and honor him.
16 With long life I will satisfy him
and show him my salvation."

Learning to Breathe
Chapter 9

I don't know what it was like to take my first breath and to feel the air rush through my lungs. I was too young the first time I took a breath. I do know what it is like to have the breath taken from my lungs. You know when you are a kid and you fall and hit your stomach and the air is knocked out from you. Some people call it a sucker punch. This is the feeling that I had when my son passed away. I felt the deep ache in my soul and I could not breathe.

There is something that happens physically when you lose a child. In the natural the child is no longer present. The dreams that were once there have now vanished into thin air and there is no remnant of their existence except for a tombstone. This was the reality that I now had to walk out every day.

I remember it had been only two days since my son's death and I was in the shower. I thought of how much my heart ached and I felt like I could not breathe. I literally felt so much pain in my chest that I could not bring myself to take another breath.

Air is the life to our bodies and during that time I did not have air to breathe. My breath had been stolen from me and I felt like I was going to die. I called out to the Lord to breathe for me. It was in those moments of my vulnerability that the Lord was ever so present. He became more real to me than I had ever experienced.

For the first time since our son had passed away I felt a deep breath fill my lungs. I was able to stand straight and breathe. In those moments I clung to the cold shower walls and cried. I felt such a release of pain as I cried out to Jesus to fill my lungs. I needed him in that moment and for the moments that were to come. I needed him for life.

I find it interesting that the very thing that my son died from was a lack of oxygen. He did not die from some strange illness he died because he could not breathe. His strong little body was in a deep sleep that caused him to forget to breathe. I knew that I did not want to die from a lack of oxygen. I had a husband and 4 children to love and enjoy. I had a life to live. I had a God that loved me so much and wanted to continue to breathe for me.

There are so many times throughout this process that I cried out to Jesus to help me breathe. Psalm 94:17-18 says, "I would have soon settled in the silence of the grave. I cried out, "I am slipping!" but your unfailing love, O Lord supported me. When doubts filled my mind, your comfort gave me renewed hope and cheer." I cried out with every part of my being on that day in the shower. It was a memory that I will forever be grateful for. I felt deep pain but it was in that pain that I felt the presence of an Almighty God. He sustained me and gave me breath. Not only did he help me breathe but he gave me hope for the future.

My heart was turned toward the Lord and I could breathe. There is something precious about the presence of Lord meeting me in the times when I need him the most. I cried out to the Lord and He answered me. He turned his heart towards me and listened to me. He came to my rescue. He heard my plea. He heard me say God if you don't show up I will die. I would love to say that this was the only time within the last few years that I have experienced such hopelessness but it was not. This was the first time that I had cried out to the Lord and He had shown up in such a beautiful way. His presence in that shower was the hope that I needed for that moment.

One of the fascinating attributes about the Lord is his ability to heal us in the midst of our pain. I was just two months after our son passed away that our Phineas had become sick with the flu. He was about 7 months old at the time and had been struggling with a fever and cough. He was very congested and having difficulty breathing. This had me on high alert because I was afraid of losing him. It was a very real emotion that I knew I had to walk through.

It had been a few months since we had lost our boy but I knew that I needed to take his living twin to the hospital he was struggling to breathe. I had to go to the ER because nothing was open at 1 am in the morning. As I got in the van to go to the hospital I began to remember the last time I was at the hospital in the early morning hours. It was two months prior that I had followed the ambulance that was transporting my son. In hopes that my son who was in the ambulance could be revived. All I could think of was if they can just get him to breathe it will be all right. I thought even if he is a vegetable at least we would still have our son. These memories were difficult to have but I knew that my living son was sick and could not breathe well so I had to take him to the hospital.

As we arrived I remember asking the Lord to show up and help me because I did not want to go in alone. I needed the Lord to be with me and help me walk through this. I went through all of the preliminary questions and paperwork. As I am filling out these form tears are running down my face because I always use to fill out paperwork for two boys not just one. This was hard.

Pain was gripping every part of my being. I finally finished with the paperwork and they led me through the doors to the ER rooms. This was a hospital that had at least 30 ER rooms and they were all empty.

It was in these few moments that the Lord showed up in a big way. Remember when I asked him to show up when I first arrived at the hospital. Well this is where He made his presence known. I recognized His peaceful presence in that ER.

As they gave me directions to the room I thought to myself I cannot do this. The room they were directing me to was the exact room that I had been in two months prior. This was the room that I last saw my Zadok. This was the same room filled with the smell of bleach and cold white walls. This was the room that I was about to enter with my sick son. I thought to myself this is a little absurd because there are other empty rooms. Then I heard the Lord remind me that I had asked him to help me through this.

I mustered up all of the strength that I could and asked Jesus to speak to me. In those moments I had a choice to make I could choose to trust that God would be present with me and reveal something important to me or I could ask them for another room. I knew that they would accommodate but I wanted to be present in those precious moments.

I sat down on the bed and tears began to roll down my cheeks. At first there were just a few and then I began to sob. The son that was present now was the identical twin brother of Zadok who passed away just a few months prior. This was uncanny to see Phineas laying there having trouble breathing knowing that his brother is now with Jesus. I could not help but remember all of those traumatic memories. I sat there and sobbed all by myself.

I wanted to embrace the heartache that was there and open myself to the Lord so He could speak hope and life into my soul. Jesus does not leave us in our pain and suffering but will bring peace if we invite him into our pain.

He began to tell me of his love for me. He told me that where death once ruled I want to bring about life. I want to begin a new life in you. Death showed up but I want to bring life again. He was present with me and carried me. The doctor came in soon after and gave Phin a breathing treatment and he was so much better. We left with some antibiotics and the next morning Phin was already showing signs of improvement.

I learned in those moments that air is vital for our physical bodies and even more so for our souls. God wants us to breathe even in the midst of our pain and heartache. He shows up and changes the atmosphere. I had such a peace as I sat through the process of embracing the pain.

Throughout our story I hope that you see a tapestry of hope that is woven through these words. God showed up in so many moments early on because I was desperately looking for Him and pressing into His voice. He is eagerly waiting for you to lean into Him and hear His sweet voice.

The Storm

Chapter 10

In the Spring of 2012 we moved from Illinois to Massachusetts. Oh what excitement filled our hearts as we began to embark on this journey. It seemed to be a far away land filled with a great opportunity to pastor a church. So we decided to seize the opportunity. We sold our home and some of our furniture and packed up the moving truck and headed to the East Coast.

We were off on an adventure that would forever change our lives. I thought that we were going there to help pastor a church and encourage some people. We had big plans for the Boston area and were ready to change the world. Those plans for big changes were not necessarily for the church but ended up being for our family.

When we moved it had only been about 8 months since our sons passing so it was really fresh. We knew that the only way to heal was to continue to experience life and allow the waves of grief to come.

Grief has many different faces and can hit at any time day or night. I have seen grief come out like a big angry bear hungry for its next meal. Then at other times it has crept in like a child tip toeing down the stairs. It comes out of left field and there is no way to prepare for the wave of emotions that occur.

I have learned that no matter where I am and what I am doing if I feel overwhelming emotion and grief come I need to begin to embrace the pain. As I embrace it I feel a peace that is so beautiful and strong.

While living in Boston we experienced one of these storms at the beach. It was called a nor'easter and it was windy, rainy and cold. Our family decided to take the day to explore our new city so we ventured out to the beach. The wind was ferocious and the air was cool. We had never been to this particular beach before so as we were driving out to the shore we began to see the intense waves. The waves were churning as if they were stuck in a circular motion. They just kept coming to shore but never fully landed on the sand before they were cycling again. There was an intensity to this storm. They didn't crash on the shore but rather kept rolling over and over.

The sea seemed to keep its distance from the shoreline. I felt like the ocean was staying away from shore because it was so powerful. The waves stayed within their boundaries and the wind continued to howl. The sky was a dreary gray and all around was the wind and the sea. This particular storm was strong and chaotic but somehow there was a peace that surrounded us that day on the shore.

In those moments as I am taking in this powerful storm my husband decides it is a good idea to walk out toward the ocean. All I could think of was he is crazy and told him to get back into the van. However, he does not listen to me and stays by the water.

My husband leaned into the wind with his hands on his head and the wind holding him upright. He did not waver or turn. He did not fall onto the sand. He stood leaning into the wind. The wind did not over take him. The waves did not come near to him. The wind kept him standing upright and it blew right around him. He was not harmed or even wet. He leaned into the storm. He embraced the difficulty and the chaos and allowed it time to pass.

The strength and the power of the wind was majestic. There was so much beauty in that moment as I watched the storm and the waves. The idea that God is ever present in our trials as well as our good times was so present in these moments. The storm did not overtake my husband. He was not shaken but rather confident and peaceful. This particular story was a representation of our experience in life up to that point.

So many times I have wanted to escape grief because it was so painful. I did not want to face it every time it would rear its ugly head. However, I realized that grief was necessary for my health both physically and mentally. I needed time to embrace and lean into the pain and let myself feel.

Leaning into the Lord is scary and frightening and very similar to my husband leaning into the storm. But oh the rewards when you lean into his strong arms. His arms that surround and bring the most incredible peace. I found peace that day as I watched my husband lean into the wind. I found such a deep rooted anchor in the Lord that my life would be taken care of. The wind was all encompassing and surrounded us but it did not harm our family.

I love in Scripture where Moses says to the Lord that if your presence does not go with us we will not move from here. Storms will come in life and they may be so intense that you cannot stand, lean into the Lord and let him hold you up. Let his strength become your strength and his comfort become your pillow. Be like Moses and tell the Lord that if you don't go with me to face this storm I don't want to go. I will not leave without the presence of the Lord because that is where the peace and power dwell.

We all face trials and we wonder Why? This is the big question that I get asked, "Why did God allow this great loss to happen to you?" My answer is a simple one, "I don't know." May seem kind of crazy but in reality I am not God nor am I going to pretend like I have some amazing theological answer. What I do know is that God is faithful and good. I know that I have learned about his heart toward me and my family and know that He has good in store for me.

His purpose for my life is greater than what I could imagine.

Just because I know the Lord doesn't mean that I won't face difficult situations. I will face them and I will turn to the Lord for his strength to walk through it. And in the end I will see the goodness of the Lord in the land where I am living.

I have truly seen God show up in the midst of my misery and take my ashes and turn them into something beautiful. He sees my life and it is beautiful to him.

I learned that day that the peace of God can be found in the chaos of the strongest storms. The Lord has so graciously promised me that I am not alone. I do not have to fear life itself.

Isaiah 43

Do not fear, for I have redeemed you;
I have summoned you by name; you are mine.
When you pass through the waters,
I will be with you;
and when you pass through the rivers,
they will not sweep over you.
When you walk through the fire,
you will not be burned;
the flames will not set you ablaze.
For I am the Lord your God,
the Holy One of Israel, your Savior.

Judah-Joy Hope
Chapter 11

It was a chilly June morning in 2013 when I woke up to the smell of coffee. Normally the smell of coffee in the morning is amazing and brings such a smile to my face. I can tell I am getting older because I enjoy that wonderful smell in the morning. Although I do enjoy coffee this particular morning I woke up and felt sick to my stomach. Just the smell made me want to throw up. It did not take me long to figure out what was going on in my body. These were all signs that I was pregnant. My husband had just gotten up and I told him I needed to go and get some soap for the shower. So off I went to the local drug store to get soap and a pregnancy test. I knew from my symptoms that morning that I was probably pregnant, but I wanted to make sure before I began to spread the news.

Once I arrived home I took the test and my intuition was correct we were once again expecting. With each pregnancy there has always been things that I have learned along the way. This pregnancy was no different and I knew heading into it there were going to be some lessons that I learned and some stretching both physically and emotionally that I would go through.

The months flew by so fast and before long I was giving birth to a beautiful baby girl. She was born in the middle of one of the coldest winters I have ever experienced.

We decided to give her the name Judah-Joy Hope. There was

something about the name of Judah that was intriguing to me. It had this strength and beauty as it rolled off of the tongue. There was a certain exuberance that arose within me as I would say the name of Judah. I researched the name and found that it meant "Praise," but I did not understand the importance of this child in my life.

There was something significant that the Lord was going to do through my child. My husband and I had asked the Lord to use our family. This desire was in us from the beginning of our marriage however, we did not understand the way in which the Lord would begin to show off his splendor in our lives. He did indeed bring healing through our daughter and continues to speak hope into our family.

When our son died we were determined that God would be glorified. Some people would often say that I was a bit crazy when I expressed my deep adoration for the Lord and for others to know Him. They would contribute my exuberance to my grief and sometimes dismiss me. This was not the case for me I had seen the Lord pick up the pieces of my life and bring me peace. All I wanted to do was share this love with those around me I was convinced that if I was going to lose a child then my story would not end there. I was determined to share our story of hope and peace.

Judah-Joy was a reminder to me of the goodness of the Lord in a land that appeared to be desolate. It was His great splendor and majesty that allowed me to see through my pain. He allowed me to see that I could hope again. I could praise Him.

In Nehemiah 12 Judah, a Levite, returned with Zerubbabel to rebuild the wall. This was significant for the people of Israel. They had been through so much desolation and now something good was going to come from such heart ache. They were rebuilding a wall and praising God for all that He had done.

Our praise rises to the Lord like a fragrant offering. It is easy to praise and worship when life is going well but when life has been broken and we are left to pick up the pieces we are faced with a decision to push through and praise or run away and hide. My heart was convinced that no matter what I experience I will choose to praise the Lord.

We are not promised tomorrow, in fact we are told that there will be tribulation, heartache, death and disease, but Jesus tells us to take heart because He has overcome the world. Jesus has met me and my family and although we lost a child He showed up in our lives with peace.

In Nehemiah they stood on the wall and proclaimed the goodness of the Lord through their praise. Nehemiah 12:31 "I led the leaders of Judah to the top of the wall and organized two large choirs to give thanks. One of the choirs proceeded southward alone on the top of the wall." These people were praising God for what He had done in their lives.

God is not the author of our pain but if we let Him, He will use it to bring healing to our lives and glory to his name. I did not know the gift that my Judah-Joy was to my life until I had given birth and began to see her life played out.

She has brought a healing to my heart that no person could have done. There are places that I have searched inside my heart that are whole now because I was able to visit that pain that was hidden. At times during my pregnancy I would have thoughts of losing this child and the pain that it would cause me and my family. In those moments the Lord would so graciously remind me to trust him.

Knowing that he had my life planned out and would carry me through every moment gave me a freedom to walk through the tough times. There is a freedom that arises within me when I know that He has and will continue to carry me. He carries my broken pieces and puts them back together.

A few short days before our baby girl was born and our oldest daughter came to us and asked if she could name her sister Joy. I thought about this request and my immediate response was "no."

Joy just seemed like a name that did not fit with what we had picked out. Then the Lord began to speak to me about my daughter Bella and the pain that she had gone through. She was only 7 years old when she lost one of her twin brothers. The Lord not only gave hope to my husband and I, He also healed my daughter.

I am realizing that the Lord shows up and brings such healing. He is the one who sees and hears us and moves on our behalf. My daughter was experiencing hope in her life and desiring to open herself up to the Lord.

When she lost her brother, it was devastating she did not understand why her brother died. She wanted to blame me and my husband and God. She was angry with the Lord because she felt abandoned and hurt. She could not wrap her little mind around how a loving God would take her baby brother from her. Those boys were her boys. She would take care of them and was very protective of them.

In those moments when my daughter was telling us about the name Joy there was something in me that came alive. I had been praying for my girl Bella that she would begin to see that God is good and allow him to take her anger. I pleaded with the Lord to move on my child's behalf. I knew that I could not force her to love the Lord but I so desperately wanted her to turn her little heart towards the Him. I wanted for her to know the Lord in a deeper way. I wanted her heart to be made whole. So I did what I thought was best and I prayed and pleaded with the Lord to move in her life.

My Bella could have picked any name and yet she chose Joy. There is a great mystery about the Lord that I saw that day. He is so involved in the details of our life. The Lord was moving that day and I needed to be still and listen to Him. He was moving through my precious child. He was stirring in her heart this joy that was contagious and beautiful.

Bella always says that the time before Judah-Joy was born was a really sad time in our family. So she thought that if we named this new child Joy that every time we said her name we would be happy because her name is happy. This is so true to this day every time that I say Judah-Joy I think of the praise given to our Savior and how He has carried me.

I have hope today only because of Jesus. He is the anchor to my soul. I can imagine in the story of Nehemiah, the beauty when Judah went with Zerubbabel and they danced and praised on the walls. The excitement of what was to come and the pure delight in the presence of God. They were entering into this time with thanksgiving and praise.

Judah-Joy Hope was born at the perfect time in our family and reminded us of an incredible joy that our family needed. It was God's abundant joy and hope that was used to continue our healing process. As a family we have seen God be gracious. We have seen his splendor in all that is good. We have seen his blessings.

Hosea 14:7 "My people will again live under my shade. They will flourish like grain and blossom like grapevines. They will be as fragrant as the wines of Lebanon." Our family has continued to blossom and find shade under the umbrella of the Lord. We have seen Him walk us through this grieving process with grace and strength. He has been our hope and our anchor. Our peace through all of the storms has been present only because our God is so gracious.

Fear Put in its Place

Chapter 12

We were getting ready to take a trip to the beach in 2015 for a little vacation. We were so looking forward to this trip. It had been planned for a few months and we were beyond excited. The condo was right on the ocean and the sweet ocean breeze would be blowing in our face with the sound of the waves crashing on the beach. This was going to be awesome.

When we arrived at the beach we spent time with the kids and unpacked our things. When you are taking 5 kids on vacation you have to pack a ton of stuffs we were quite busy getting settled. Our vacation was so beautiful and came at the perfect time for our family we were excited to rest at the beach.

As we were getting the kids to bed the first night we put them all down except the baby. She had just turned a year old and was so incredibly perfect. In her first year of life I had her sleep with us. She would sleep in the middle of my husband and I. I would not get much sleep and neither would he. This was my way of coping with my anxiety and fear. We never really talked about it except in a joking way.

I had no idea the amount of stress this decision had put on me and my husband. I was just trying to cope with my fear of losing another child. Our daughter did have a crib and a room. However, I could not allow myself to lay her down to sleep at night. My thought was if I lay her down I will not see her alive again. I was so afraid. I was so afraid of losing something that was so precious. I felt like I would never be able to overcome this fear. It had gripped me at my core. I felt like it was the new normal for me. I had already lived 3 years with this fear and it had taken root in my soul.

My baby would take naps in her crib in the afternoon when it was daylight but would never sleep at night in her crib. I kept all of this fear, stress, and anxiety a secret because I did not want others to see my weakness. I felt that if I shared my struggle I would be categorized as broken. I didn't know how to wrestle through the pain and use my weakness as a platform to share Jesus. I could share the hope that I found through the pain but the internal wrestle was a different kind of transparency.

The fear that I had dealt with since August 18th, 2011was because of the loss of our son. However, it had crept into ever aspect of my life. My fears became irrational. There were few things in my life that I was not willing to let go of and this was one of them. I was not going to let my 1 year old sleep by herself in her safe crib. I had already lost a baby to SIDS I was determined to not lose another one. Even as I write these words it still feels so foreign to me. I allowed this fear to overwhelm me and guide my decisions when it came to my kids and other areas of my life.

There were times over those first few years that I would wake up with panic attacks. It would happen 3-4 times a week. These panic attacks were very common for me and no matter how much I asked the Lord to help I still struggled with them.

I would jump out of bed and run to check on my other kids. I would take my hand and place it on my kid's chest to see if it would go up and down. If it did then I knew that they were still alive and breathing. This was a sick and disturbing cycle that I went through night after night. It was controlling me and I was struggling. I was struggling alone.

This cycle finally broke when we were on this particular vacation at the beach and I laid my baby girl down to sleep. I put her in her pack and play and I walked away. I remember walking into the bedroom at the condo and hearing the crashing waves. The wind was gently blowing through the opened patio door and I just listened. I listened for that peace. I listened for that sweet voice that was telling me that it was ok. It was ok to walk through loss and fear of the future. It was ok to trust Jesus in this area that was still so tender. It was ok to desire more for myself and my family and not have the answers of how to get rid of this fear. I sat on the bed and just listened.

This is a time that if I am quiet I go back to it in my mind and I feel peace. I feel the presence of the Lord and His sweet goodness. Jesus knew that I had a soft spot for the beach and if He was going to speak something to me about letting go of fear it had to be in a place where I was comfortable and at peace. The beach was that place....

As I laid her down I remember saying, "Jesus I trust you with my baby." This was a big deal for me because I did not want to trust Jesus with my baby. I was too scared to trust Him.

Earlier in the day as I was talking with my husband he asked me this question, "what is the worst that can happen?" These words were not words that I wanted to hear. I did not want to face the possibility of losing another child, but I heard my husband's heart in his questioning. He wanted me to face the worst thing that could happen in my mind. As I asked myself this question I was able to face the fear of loss. Sometimes we can get so focused on the loss that we forget that we can live.

The loss I experienced was great but I knew that Jesus would walk with me through it. I knew that his presence would be with me if I ever had to face it again. I laid my baby down and said, "Jesus I trust you with my baby." I knew that the Lord would teach me how to trust Him and walk this out.

I believe that something broke in the spiritual realm that night. I never had a panic attack after that night. I slept through the night peacefully and without fear. It was amazing the healing that took place in my soul as I began to trust Jesus. Fear no longer had a foothold in my soul.

There were definitely some pros to sleeping without a one year old in my bed. My husband was more than thrilled that he was able to sleep through the night without a baby waking him up. I was able to get sleep for the first time in three years. Three years was a long time to not sleep through the night because of fear and panic.

Fear, panic and anxiety are real emotions. I learned through this process that I was dealing with PTSD. I had never wanted to admit that I was struggling with this because I did not want to look weak. I did not want to be labelled or have to go on medication to numb the pain.

I felt like there were so many emotions tied to all of it and if I could just untangle it, I would be ok. This was a long process for me to walk through. In my few short years of walking this path, I have realized that there is power in sharing my story, even the daily struggles. There has been more freedom as I have shared my story and the struggles that I faced.

Our Arrow

Chapter 13

"Behold children are a heritage and gift from the Lord, The fruit of the womb a reward. Like arrows in the hand of a warrior, So are the children of one's youth. How blessed is the man whose quiver is filled with them; They will not be ashamed when they speak with their enemies at the gates."

Psalm 127:3-4

It was a cool March morning in 2018 and I was a few days late. I had been on this natural method of birth control that uses a calendar. If anyone suggests for you to use an APP to keep track of your period and when you are ovulating tell them, "no thank you." This is how our latest little one came to be. I was using this app that had been spot on for almost two years except for this time.

I should tell you that I am not good at math it is not my

strong suit. I thought for sure that we were in the clear according to my app, only to find out that I was indeed pregnant with our seventh child.

When I found out I was pregnant I had taken my van in to get the tires rotated so I took the pregnancy test in the bathroom of the tire business. Then I took another one because I was not 100% sure that the first one was correct. Then I took 2 more when I got home. I was in shock that I was in fact pregnant. God had other plans for our family that year and it included a new baby. I love it when God shows up and totally messes with my plans.

During my last pregnancy I decided to take time to finish this book. The following paragraphs are some of my thoughts that I wrote down.

"Little one you may not have been in my plans but you were in my dreams. I did not know that you were needed in our life. Your little life was to be formed in the hands of the Lord and given to us in the late fall. You will be an arrow in your daddy's quiver. You will be strength to this family and hope for our future. The dreams and desires that God has for you are perfect. I am over the moon excited for you to be born.

Of course, my emotions are all over the place right now and I am trying to keep some calm in my soul. It continues to be an amazing challenge to walk out this journey. I have been thinking of you baby non-stop. Thinking of all of the changes that will take place over the next 8 months. I don't know that I am prepared to handle all of it and then I remember that I don't have to do it alone. This pregnancy and you precious little one are going to be different.

I think that it is not just trusting Jesus with this pregnancy but to look fear in the face and know that it is defeated. It was defeated on the cross and it is defeated today. To actually walk into the room and the fear flee. It was not because I had now faced my fears and was ready to embrace the unknown but rather I was prepared to trust Jesus in a deeper way. Fearless. . . what does it mean to be fearless? This is where my heart wants to stay fearless."

To walk through what my husband and I have walked through and then to fully embrace this pregnancy will take courageous bravery. To have the heart of a lion and to run into battle knowing that the outcome will be as an overcomer is the cry of my heart.

I am fully prepared to walk out this pregnancy and raise this child with fearless tenacity. To be fearless in life takes a strength that I do not have but I know someone who does.

As I sit here and ponder the big issues of our world I am realizing we are all waiting for something. Some of us may be waiting on a call from the doctor or the arrival of a new baby. Some may be waiting on an answer from the Lord or call about a job. Waiting plays a big part in our lives. I would say that much of my life has been found in the waiting. This baby that I am about to give birth to is a Sweet Kiss from Heaven. He has given me the ability to open my heart and trust Jesus where pain and doubt once existed."

I learned so much in this season of waiting. I have this app on my phone and it tells me what happens with the baby each week. I remember counting the weeks as they went by and wishing that time would go by faster. It was 5 weeks, then 8 weeks, then 13 weeks and then 29 weeks. I felt him kick and roll in my belly.

There were times when I felt like an alien had taken over my body and become the master. I saw my clothes get too small and the stretch marks return and become more visable. I think I had felt every symptom of pregnancy this time around. The symptoms usually only lasted for a few days. I am trying to embrace every moment because I know that this is my last one.

It had been so incredible to see arms go from little buds to full arms with ten little fingers and toes. There has been this sweetness that has occurred during this waiting period. As I watched him grow I am in awe of the goodness of the Lord and His love for me.

I would not have chosen to be in this season of waiting but I am finding such beauty in this process. The intricate detail of a baby being formed on the inside is a reflection of what is going on in my life. This journey has been surprising and unique to my family. We have seen the Lord care for our family in such extravagant ways. There are times when I think God has been so good how could it get any better. Then I remember that His very nature is good. How can He be anything but good to me?

As a family we have walked through some traumatic events in our life. I have given birth to 7 children. We have walked through the death of a child and the tremendous sadness and despair that comes along with loss. I personally have seen God's hand in all of it. He has been so present in my brokenness and pain. He has never left me to wonder "God where are you?" There has not been one moment when I was alone. He was Always there. Always ready for a word to comfort my aching heart. Always there to heal a little more of my brokenness.

Here in the presence of the Lord is life. He moves in ways that are far beyond my grasp. He speaks so tenderly to me it is as if He is sitting beside me. Life does not always make sense. There is pain and heartache, desperation and horrible tragedies that occur every day. I cannot make sense of it all or even begin to understand, but I have a God who says, "will you trust me in this? Will you ask me again for those specific needs in your life? Will you let me be a part of you healing? Will you give me full control of your thoughts, your heart, your emotion and your will? Allow me to be what you need in that moment and if it changes it will be my pleasure to move into what you need. I am the Great I Am. Will you come to me and boldly ask for what you need?"

November 15th 2018 our Benjamin Arrow was born without complications. He came a few weeks early at a hefty 8 pounds and a few ounces. He is the perfect baby boy. I look at my son and am amazed at the goodness of the Lord. I feel as though the goodness of the Lord is wrapped up in this little guy.

Praise be to my God who does not leave me alone to wallow in my sadness. Praise be to my God who continues to draw me into His presence. Praise be to my God who calls me out my darkness and leads me by the quiet still waters. Praise be to my God who redeems everything the enemy has stolen.

Message in a Bottle

Chapter 14

Every year on August 18th we celebrate our sweet Zadok. Over the years we have done so many different things to remember him. We have gone to the mountains and hiked up to the highest peak and left flowers on the mountain side. Another year we travelled to Dinosaur Valley and hiked along the river and watched our flowers flow down stream. Then other years we have celebrated him by going out to a favorite restaurant and laughing with the kids. Each year it is something different but our goal is to always thank the Lord for our precious gift and celebrate his little life as a family.

In August of 2016 we celebrated Zadok's day at the beach in Delaware. We made cards and wrote down our story of loss and hope. We put it into a wine bottle and made sure it was sealed nice and tight. We left it with a friend who was to take it out into the ocean and drop it in. We were told that my dad's friend had a fishing boat and they would make trips out into the ocean all of the time. We were so excited about this and the adventure that our bottle would go on over the next few months or even years.

One Friday evening in January 2020 I received an email from a lady who told me that she had found our bottle and that she was sorry for our loss. As I was reading tears were flooding down my cheeks. Her words brought comfort and pain all at the same time. I could not believe what I was reading our bottle had been found and the story been shared.

This lady and I went back and forth a few times with emails. I asked her where she was located and how she found the bottle. I was very intrigued at this point because I wanted to know where the bottle was picked up. She told me that she had recently purchased a boat and found the bottle laying there.

As my conversation continued with this lady I briefly told her that it was our twin that had passed away. She then began to share with me about her friend who happened to be helping her clean her newly acquired boat that day. It was actually the friend who found the bottle as they were cleaning. She said that it was the one year anniversary of when she had lost her twins.

I was absolutely speechless at this point. I could not believe that this bottle had been found and that some random stranger had lost her twins and it was their anniversary of the loss. Her friend mentioned that she had heard of our story and thought if this woman can go on then I can have hope for my future as well.

The impact of my story was affecting a woman who lived many miles away from me and my family. This precious woman who had lost her babies was given a little glimmer of hope as she looked at our precious bottle and the pictures.

He had felt the tangible presence of the Lord. I am reminded of the story of Hagar when she called God, "El Roi the God who sees me." What an incredible God I serve that sees me and connects me with a woman who needs to be seen and loved.

My kids and I looked through the pictures that she had emailed us and were reminiscing of our time at the beach. They loved looking at the little pictures they had drawn. We could not believe that we were reconnecting with a piece of our heart from years ago.

I am astonished that the Lord would use a simple thing like a message in a bottle to bring hope to someone else years later. The bottle never made it out into the ocean. It remained in the corner on that small fishing boat for 3 ½ years. It had been rained on and abandoned and possibly looked at as trash. Then one day it was time for that bottle to be found and when it was God began to speak.

I think that God had a plan and purpose for that bottle all along. It was never meant to go out on an adventure into the big ocean. The purpose of that bottle was to sit and patiently wait. It was to encourage a sweet mamma as she mourned the loss of her children.

God has an incredible plan and purpose for our lives and for yours. We may not see the details as we are walking through the dark seasons but there is hope. Psalm 23 is one of my favorite passages of Scripture because it brings such hope and peace.

> "God my shepherd! I don't need a thing. You have bedded me down in the lush meadows, you find me quiet pools to drink from. True to your word, you let me catch my breath and send me in the right direction. Even when the way goes through Death Valley, I am not afraid when you walk at my side. Your trusty shepherd's crook makes me feel secure." Holy Bible, The Message

God you have been by my side through it all. Even when I felt alone you have always walked beside me and carried me at times when I could not walk. You oh my God have exceeded my expectations and given me hope. You have grown my faith and given me peace as I trust you for more. God you have been good to me.

The Lord is patient and compassionate and His love is endearing. He has plans that are good for you. He has a way of preparing a table for you in the midst of your enemies and your cup will run over. He brings a peace as you walk through dark times and He constantly reminds you that you are not alone.

The Goodness of my God
Chapter 15

Tonight will be my last chapter. This is it. It is kind of ironic because tonight marks the eve of my son's birthday. Eight years ago tonight I was sitting in a hospital room waiting for my twins to arrive. I was waiting as the contractions were coming and my body was doing what it was created to do, birth my boys. I remember it so well as I sat there in the hospital bed with monitors on me and on my babies. My husband was sitting across from me anxiously awaiting the arrival of his boys. I was waiting.

The writing of this book has been one of those tasks that has been so challenging for me to accomplish. I have wanted to write this book ever since my son passed away and yet I have found it to be so difficult to complete. I have started and stopped many times over the years for a variety of reasons. The reason is because it is so painful to relive each of these memories. Although it has been painful I have also found healing and hope each time I write.

I titled this chapter the goodness of the Lord because He has been so good to me. I have seen His hand move in my life and I have felt His presence in such a tangible way. I can't help but remember the Lord's gracious kindness to me as I have walked through the loss of my son. He has been good. I remember the beautiful moments that I had with my babies.

They say hindsight is 20/20. As I look back at my life I can remember the Lord moving and showing His goodness in so many amazing ways.

When I was 5 my family had found ourselves with little food and no money. We decided to go for a walk that day in our neighborhood. Upon our return there were over 10 bags of groceries on our front door step. There was a letter in one of the bags and it said, "we wanted to bless your family with some food." We did not know who it came from but we sure were thankful for the food. I remember telling my mom that God would provide for our family and He did. He showed us His goodness that day.

As I continue to recount the goodness of the Lord I can't help but get excited about all that the Lord has done and continues to do in my life. It was last year about this time that my husband and I found out that we were pregnant. This time I was completely shocked. We were on this path of not having any more children. We were very happy with our 5 on earth and 1 in heaven. Although we were not planning on this baby God showed us His goodness again.

We were not expecting to see God's goodness in the form of another child but He blessed us with the most amazing gift. There has been a peace and joy that has entered our home and family. We look at our baby boy and see God smiling. Our baby has become a sweet kiss from heaven to our family. We are so in love with him.

When Arrow was born it was as though a new world was created for me. I had a new perspective on life and loss. I could see life in a new light. There was such a peace about my new son. His life was covered in fearless tenacity. I look at him and I see God's redemptive work in my life.

Arrow you are the goodness of the Lord wrapped up in a package just for me. I would like to think that Arrow was created just for me and my family but I know that God has a plan for him.

The goodness of the Lord has always been evident in my life but it was not until I had lost so much that I began to realize how good and gracious the Lord has been to me. I know that through my pain I have focused on seeing God move. We live in this fallen world that is full of sin. There are some circumstances that are out of my control. As much as I would like to control all of my life I cannot. However, there is a trust that I have had to learn over these past 8 years. I have to trust that God has a plan for me even if the plan does not turn out the way I had envisioned.

The goodness of the Lord is not dependent on God giving me everything that I want. His goodness is a part of His nature. He is good no matter what my circumstances may be.

My circumstances do not change the goodness of the Lord they simply allow me to see with eyes wide open Him moving on my behalf. There are many things that I have learned over the years but the most valuable lesson I have learned is that God does not change. He is constant. If He says that He will provide and make a way then He will do it. My job is to stay connected to Him. I need to stay open and vulnerable to him moving and speaking. There are times that I need to embrace the pain of the moment and then hand it over to Him. I have had to trust Him with my children, my pregnancies, my finances. He has never once failed me or my family.

His goodness and His love go hand in hand. He is good because that is his nature. He cannot go against His very nature. My life has been filled with heart ache and joy and my family has chosen to trust in the goodness of the Lord.

As I close out this chapter I am trusting in a faithful, good, loving, gracious God to move in the midst of my pain. I am believing that He will do what He said He would do. I am trusting that as I raise my kids He will give me wisdom and grace. I am desiring that this book will bring hope to those walking through grief. I am longing for the day when I will be in Heaven seeing my son and worshipping my God. I am living for today as I continue to share our story and embrace the pain of losing my son. I am sitting here tonight praying that God will wrap His amazing arms around you and heal the pain that is in the depths of your soul.

May the God who lives and moves invade your heart and may you know the love that He has for you. May you see the goodness of the Lord in the land where you live. May you feel his presence and see Him move. Praying that you will be able to embrace the pain of life and then release it to the one who longs to hold the pieces of your heart and put them back together. Know that you are loved friend. Know that there is a God who cares about your heart. Know that there is a family in Texas who is praying that you will know you are loved. There is a story of redemption and hope that come out of your life if you will allow the living God a place to dwell.

Throughout our story I hope that you see a tapestry of hope that is woven through these words. God showed up in so many moments early on because I was desperately looking for Him and pressing into His voice. He is eagerly waiting for you to lean into Him and hear His sweet voice.

"The Lord bless you and keep you the Lord make his face shine upon you and be gracious to you the Lord look upon you with favor and give you peace."

My Prayer for You

Watch this short video of gratitude and a prayer for you! https://youtu.be/LHCYGFI5zhQ

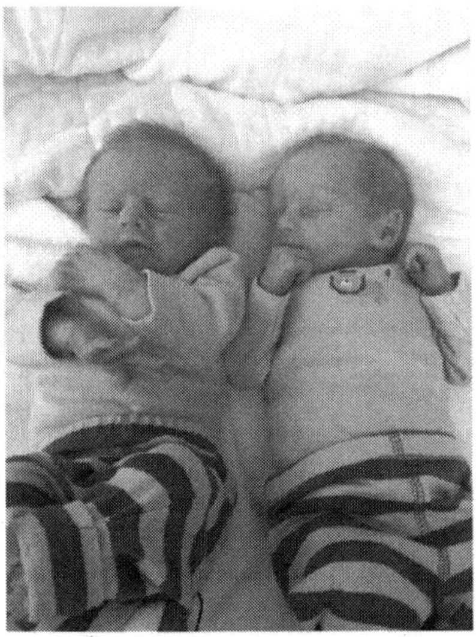

Phineas and Zadok

Zadok's grave

About The Author

Jenn Winn

Jenn Winn is a wife and mom to 7 beautiful children. she married her college sweetheart in 2001 and became a mom just a few years later. Jenn and her family have walked through the loss of their son and found healing in their relationship with Jesus. Jenn has a desire to minister to those who have lost and help them find healing and hope through their journey. As a mom she knows that her children are her strength and joy. Her desire is that all would come to know the love and grace of Jesus.

Get in contact with me by email at jnnwinn@yahoo.com. (That's right, no "e".) You can also find me on Facebook and Instagram at Lilacs in November.

Made in the USA
Middletown, DE
08 May 2024

54050816R00046